D0118741

Cyber Citizenship and Cyber Safety™

Intellectual Property

Jeri Freedman

rosen publishing's
rosen central®

New York

Published in 2008 by The Rosen Publishing Group, Inc.
29 East 21st Street, New York, NY 10010

Library of Congress Cataloging-in-Publication Data

Freedman, Jeri.
Intellectual property / Jeri Freedman.—1st ed.
    p. cm.—(Cyber citizenship and cyber safety)
Includes bibliographical references.
ISBN-13: 978-1-4042-1348-7 (library binding)
1. Intellectual property—United States—Juvenile literature.
2. Copyright and electronic data processing—United States—Juvenile literature. 3. Computers—Law and legislation—United States—Juvenile literature. I. Title.
KF2980.F74 2008
346.7304'8—dc22

                                                    2007027076

Manufactured in Malaysia

Contents

Introduction

It is important to use computers and the Internet safely and responsibly. The Internet is a worldwide network (connected group) of computers that can communicate with each other digitally. A lot of information is available to you on the Internet. But the fact that you can access that information does not mean it is proper or safe to use it any way you want. A lot of the music, videos, and written material on the Internet was created by individuals or companies, and it belongs to them. There is a right way and a wrong way to use such material. As a computer user, it is your job to know the difference. Penalties for misusing online material can be serious.

Property is something that someone owns. We all understand what it means to own physical property, such as a computer or a bicycle. We have strong feelings of ownership about physical property, and we expect the law to punish people who steal things. Creative works and inventions that are the result of original ideas are also property. Because this property is created with the mind, or intellect, it is called intellectual property.

People who create original books, computer games, songs, or movies feel strongly about their intellectual property, too. Just as you can sell your physical property to someone else, the creator of an intellectual work can sell a copy of it to someone else. The person or company that owns the work will fight to protect it from being stolen. When it comes to protecting intellectual property, the law grants certain rights of ownership to the creator. These are called intellectual property rights.

Digital technologies have changed the face of intellectual property rights. The Internet and devices such as computers with CD (compact disc) and DVD (digital video disc) readers and writers now make it much easier than ever before to obtain and share works created by others. However, the fact that it is easy to access intellectual property does not mean it is OK to use it without permission, or give it away to others.

The most famous intellectual property rights case of recent times is that of Napster. Founded in 1999, Napster was a service that allowed people to share music files. To use the service, users sent music file indexes from their home computers to the Napster computers, called servers. Then, other Napster users could search the servers to locate and

Devices such as iPods are forcing recording companies to approach copyright issues in new ways. For example, some companies no longer enforce global copyright restrictions on their digital music.

copy, or download, the music files they liked. The problem with this system was that Napster did not own the rights to the music it was distributing this way. The musicians who created the music and the record companies that produced it owned the rights to it. The Recording Industry Association of America (RIAA), whose members are the major record companies, sued Napster for misusing their properties. The RIAA won, and Napster was forced to shut down. (It has since reopened as a service where users can download music for a fee.) The Napster case brought attention to the issues relating to intellectual property rights.

This book explains what intellectual property is and examines intellectual property rights. It explains what types of use are allowed under the law and the penalties for misusing intellectual property. You'll also read about the steps that companies are taking to protect their intellectual property and the new laws and technologies that are being developed.

Chapter 1

Intellectual Property in a Digital World

This chapter looks at intellectual property rights and some of the ways in which digital technology has affected them.

What Is a Copyright?

In the nondigital world, intellectual property such as music, movies, computer games, and books is protected by a copyright. A copyright is a set of legal rights that are valid in the United States and in other countries. In its simplest form, a copyright is the legal right to copy a work such as a song, movie, or book. In printed versions of such a work, a copyright is indicated by the copyright symbol (©) or the word "Copyright" and the year. But even when neither of these is present, original creations are still protected by copyright law.

This is so because of the Berne Convention (*see boxed inset, pages 10–11*), an international agreement stating that a copyright is automatically granted to an author as soon as a work is created.

The copyright stays in existence until it expires or is transferred to someone else. Copyright includes the right to produce the material in other forms. For instance, you can't use a poem someone has written as lyrics for a song without that person's permission. Using intellectual property without the copyright holder's permission is called copyright infringement. Legal penalties for copyright infringement may include fines or imprisonment. If you infringe on copyright while on the job or in school, the punishment could also include being fired or expelled.

If copyright is automatically granted, you might ask, why should an author bother to register his or her work? You must register your copyright with the U.S. Copyright Office before you are legally permitted to bring a lawsuit to enforce it. The author can register a copyright at any time, but registering it in a timely manner may make it easier to win a copyright infringement case. Registration within three months of the work's publication date—or at least before any copyright infringement actually begins—makes it much easier to sue an infringer. More specifically, timely registration indicates to a court that your copyright is valid.

Under copyright law today, the author is the only one with the right to make copies of his or her work. (The author may

The first U.S. copyright protections for books, maps, and other materials were signed into law in 1790.

also pass on this right to his or her heirs or another party, called an assign.) This right stays in effect for the author's lifetime plus seventy years. This is true whether the work is sold or given away free.

After the copyright expires, the work is said to be in the "public domain." Works in the public domain can be reproduced by anyone, but only the original work of the author is in the public domain. This is very important in

Protecting Intellectual Property in the Past

In the Middle Ages, people in Europe lived a feudal life. A village or town was ruled by a lord, and everyone else served him in return for protection. During this time, most creative works were produced by artists who were supported by a patron. The patron was usually a noble person who supported the artist financially. This allowed the artist to avoid field labor or military service and devote himself instead to creating musical, literary, or artistic works. The patron maintained control over the works the artist created. For example, anyone who wanted to play a composition created by the musician needed the permission of the patron.

However, by the 1400s, feudal life had begun to give way to a different system. Individual craftsmen and merchants lived in towns and earned significant money, which they used to purchase works of art and books. Books were still considered luxury items during this time, as copies of books were produced one at a time, each one written by hand. Then, around 1450, a German printer named Johannes Gutenberg invented movable type. Movable type uses pieces of metal with letters on them that are set in rows to spell out words. Ink is placed on the type, and paper is placed over it. Then a device is pressed down on the paper to imprint the words onto the page. The movable type printing press was as revolutionary in its day as digital technology is in ours. After Gutenberg, books could be printed over and over relatively inexpensively.

This engraving shows the first printing press, invented by Johannes Gutenberg.

Since publishers paid authors for their works, they wanted to protect their investment. The easy production of books prompted publishers to seek legal protection against people copying their works. In 1710, for the first time, the British Statute of Anne granted authors ownership rights to their works. Such early copyright laws applied only to the country in which they were passed. The first widespread laws went into effect in 1886. That year, many European nations signed the Berne Convention. By signing this document, they agreed to recognize that the copyright on a creative work belonged to the author, even if he or she lived in one of the other countries. Interestingly, the United States did not sign this agreement until 1989.

relation to uploading and downloading music. You could, for instance, record your own version of a song written in the nineteenth century and upload it to the Internet without violating the law. This is the case with many Christmas carols, for instance. However, a recording of a particular band or orchestra playing that song is probably protected by copyright.

Digital Technology and Intellectual Property

In the past, copying someone's work meant physically producing a copy. This usually required a lengthy or complicated mechanical process. To illegally reprint a book, for example, you had to set type and print it on a printing press. Duplicating a

Inexpensive materials and digital technology make it easy to mass-produce DVDs, like those seen here.

movie meant you had to get hold of a reel of film and have a photo developer physically make more reels of film just like it. These processes were complicated, time consuming, and often very expensive. Digital technology has changed all that. It provides easy access to intellectual property, and it allows for quick and easy ways of copying intellectual property.

"You can find anything on the Internet." You've probably heard this, and it isn't far from the truth. With more than a billion people connected to the Internet in 2007 and over 100 million Web sites, it isn't hard to find anything you're looking for, whether it's protected by a copyright or not. And the simple fact is that for many types of intellectual property, it is no longer necessary to make a physical copy to use the material. Songs, videos, and written articles can now be accessed readily on a home computer. It is also easy to transfer digital information directly from one computer to another—or from a computer to an electronic viewing or listening device. Digital technology has also made it easier to reproduce or duplicate (copy) original works for distribution. No longer is it necessary to create records in a factory. Now anyone can copy an audio or video file on his or her home computer to a compact disc (CD) or digital video disc (DVD). At less than a dollar apiece for the discs, it's possible to make copies for friends—or copies to sell—more easily than ever before.

Intellectual Property Rights: Protecting Works

Why do we need intellectual property rights? The most obvious answer to this question is that intellectual property rights allow the creator to make a living from his or her creations. If there were no way to make a living by creating movies, books, games, or music, not many people would bother to create them. It's

Mariah Carey has been one of the top-selling singers since 1990. Such popular artists stand to lose a lot of money from digital copyright infringement.

true that some people create intellectual works as a hobby, but to create, manufacture, and distribute the best products usually requires many people and many hours of work. Even intellectual works like books, which can be created by a single person, require the author to have enough income to be able to spend his or her time writing them. It is important to understand that there is a lot more to intellectual property than the medium it is delivered on. It may seem as if a music file costs nothing to produce because it is downloaded without physical form. However, when you reproduce copyrighted songs or videos from a friend's computer and use them, you are essentially stealing. It is not that different from stealing a CD or DVD from a store.

The efforts of many people and a lot of expensive equipment were necessary to make those products—and that costs money. Because many people want to have these products, they are valuable. And because they are valuable, the people and companies that create them want to protect their value with ownership rights.

Intellectual Property Rights: Protecting Ideas

The reasons for protecting a song, book, or movie are easy to see. It may be harder to understand why you can't just use people's words or ideas when they are not written down as part of a commercial product. If a journalist for *Wired* magazine writes an online article you like, why can't you just copy what that person says and post it on your weblog? There are two reasons. The first is ethical—that is, it relates to what is right and wrong. Taking credit for something someone else thought of is unethical. It's OK to tell other people someone's ideas. After all, that's probably why that person posted them on the Internet to begin with. However, that person deserves credit. The second reason is financial. The magazine or Web site on which the information is published owns the rights to that material. In the case of a magazine, it is paying the salary of the author and the cost of running the magazine and maintaining the Web site. It has the right to sell reprints of the article to make money. Or it may want to use the article to get people to visit the Web site because it is getting advertising income by posting ads there. Or it may be posting the article to get people to come to the Web site in the hopes that they will want to subscribe to the magazine. The bottom line is that information, even in a nonphysical form, is worth money, and that information does not belong to you.

Chapter 2

Using Intellectual Property Fairly

There are acceptable ways of using copyrighted material. Unfortunately, there is no clear-cut definition of what is acceptable. Instead, U.S. copyright law has guidelines for what is called "fair use."

Fair Use

Much depends on the context of the use. To help you determine fair use, the guidelines consider the type of work, the purpose for which the work is being used, how much of the copyrighted work is being used, and the effect of that use on the market for the work. Some of the key aspects of fair use include the following:

- The material being copied must be for noncommercial use. In other words, it can't be sold either in print or electronic form. It must be for personal use. Thus, you can't copy a computer game and sell it.
- Usually, you may use only part of the work. Copying an entire work, such as a whole book or CD, can sometimes be fair use, but only in certain cases.
- In most cases, you cannot violate the terms of the license agreement. For example, many software companies allow users to make one backup copy of a disc for safekeeping but do not allow users to install the purchased program on more than one computer.

Key to fair use is the user's intent—why he or she is copying the material. It is not acceptable to duplicate a CD in order to sell the copy and make a buck. However, it is acceptable to make a copy of a song to load onto your MP3 player to listen to on the ride to school. Your intent for making the copy is personal use. In addition, it's acceptable to quote passages from copyrighted works in a book or music review or school paper. In this case, clearly the intent is not to distribute the work itself but to discuss it. However, if you quote long passages from a book, you generally need the permission of the copyright owner.

Digital Rights Management

Companies are taking steps to protect their copyrights by making it more difficult for users to make copies of CDs and DVDs. Game, music, and movie manufacturers are installing complicated software on their discs to prevent users from making and giving out copies. This type of electronic protection is called digital rights management (DRM). The manufacturers claim that DRM protection is necessary in order to stop piracy. Users, however, claim that such technologies keep them from making backup copies in case expensive discs get damaged. In addition, the copy protection software used on computer games sometimes interferes with the operation of the computer. So the problem remains: How is it possible to protect both the copyright holder and the user?

Some material was created so long ago that it is no longer protected by copyright. Material published before 1923 is in the public domain. This means that anyone may publish that material. It does not mean that you can publish it without acknowledging the author, however. Whenever you use material from another source, you should cite the author and publisher of the material so that the source is clear. Failure to do so, as discussed in chapter 3, is plagiarism.

Freeware and Shareware

Two classes of software exist that you can use without infringing (or violating) the copyright. These are called shareware and freeware. Freeware is software that the creators make available free of charge to other users, either to enjoy or to use as part of their own programs. An example of this type of software is fan-created files of add-on scenery for flight simulation games.

Freeware and shareware allow you and your friends to try out new games without having to pay a fee up-front.

Two common types of free programs are (1) additions to games or complete games that fans create and wish to share with other fans and (2) utilities, or software programs that make using other programs easier. This software is specifically published to improve the group experience of those who use the programs. The creator's goal is to get recognition and approval rather than make money. The most famous example of freeware is the Linux computer operating system, originally developed by Linus Torvalds. Releasing the software as freeware

Linus Torvalds, inventor of the Linux computer operating system. Torvalds originally developed Linux for his master degree thesis at the University of Helsinki, Finland.

has allowed a vast number of people in the computing community to contribute improvements to the software. That is why Linux is one of the most popular operating systems for businesses today.

Although there is no charge for freeware, the creators of freeware may limit how you can use it. For example, they may require programs that are created with it to also be free. So if you use a freeware program to create software, be sure you understand the terms under which you are allowed to use it.

Shareware, in contrast to freeware, is not free. Shareware is software that you do not have to pay for before using. You can download it to try it out, but you are expected to pay for it if you like it and plan to keep using it. For example, someone might make a computer game and allow you to download it and try it out. If you keep it on your computer, you will be asked to pay for it. Sometimes, shareware programs are limited demo versions of complete programs that are only

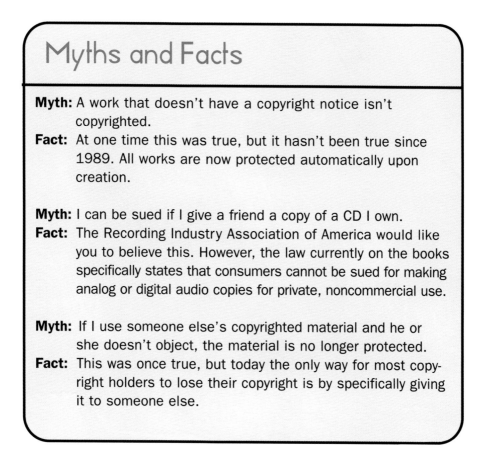

Myths and Facts

Myth: A work that doesn't have a copyright notice isn't copyrighted.

Fact: At one time this was true, but it hasn't been true since 1989. All works are now protected automatically upon creation.

Myth: I can be sued if I give a friend a copy of a CD I own.

Fact: The Recording Industry Association of America would like you to believe this. However, the law currently on the books specifically states that consumers cannot be sued for making analog or digital audio copies for private, noncommercial use.

Myth: If I use someone else's copyrighted material and he or she doesn't object, the material is no longer protected.

Fact: This was once true, but today the only way for most copyright holders to lose their copyright is by specifically giving it to someone else.

available after you receive a special code that allows you to "unlock" the full program. Other shareware is offered on the honor system. In this case, you are simply asked to pay for the program if you like it. In either case, the program itself is still the property of the person who created it. It is wrong to continue to use a shareware program without paying for it. It is also disrespectful of the person who created it.

Chapter 3

Misusing Intellectual Property

The misuse of intellectual property occurs when people use copyrighted material improperly or without the owner's permission. Sometimes, the misuse is done on purpose; other times, the misuse is accidental. This chapter looks at the misuse of intellectual property and the consequences of misuse.

Digital Pirates

When people take intellectual property that belongs to others and sell it, this is called piracy. Piracy is stealing. Many pirates are professionals, as is the case with groups that deliberately make many copies of video games, music CDs, and movie DVDs in order to sell them. Illegal copies of CDs and DVDs

In 2007, China cracked down on intellectual property piracy. Here, authorities use a bull-dozer to destroy some of the 584,000 illegal CDs they confiscated.

are called bootleg copies. However, piracy may also include copying a computer program, music, or movie CD and giving it to someone else—something many people do all the time.

It is important to understand that when you buy a software, music, or movie CD or DVD, you are usually buying the right to install it on one computer or to use it yourself. Most software comes with a license agreement that explains the ways you are allowed to use it. If you make copies of CDs or DVDs and give them to your friends, you are committing piracy. Similarly, if you install a CD or DVD that is licensed for one computer on multiple computers, you are also committing piracy. You may never be caught or brought to court for this type of piracy, but it is piracy just the same.

The Cost of Digital Piracy

The industry watchdogs that track piracy assume that each bootlegged copy is a lost sale. Using this method, the Software & Information Industry Association (SIIA) estimates that the software industry loses about $11 to $12 billion to piracy every year. The biggest losses come from professional pirates who work in Asia, especially China. However, even in the United States, the rate of piracy is high. The SIIA estimates that about 25 percent of all software used in the United States is pirated. This is largely due to people installing software on more computers than is allowed.

The Recording Industry Association of America estimates that the recording industry loses $4.2 billion every year to piracy worldwide. The Motion Picture Association of America estimates losses of $18.2 billion annually due to pirated DVDs and illegal Internet downloads. About $1.3 billion of this occurs in the United States. If you make copies of your CDs and DVDs to share or install your programs on friends' computers, it is both wrong and illegal. Beyond this, you are the one who pays the price for piracy: in the end, companies raise the price of their products to cover their losses.

Why Shouldn't I?

You may be asking yourself why you should pay for a disc if you can get it free. After all, buying CDs and DVDs is expensive. However, using illegal copies of software, music CDs, or DVDs creates a number of problems in the long run:

It increases the prices that companies charge for such items in the future.

There is a great chance of getting a computer virus (a program that destroys data or impedes the performance of your computer). This can happen because the friend who makes you a copy doesn't know that his or her computer has a virus on it, and the virus is transferred to your computer along with the file.

You cannot get technical support if you have a problem with a pirated program.

If you buy bootleg software, CDs, or DVDs, you may find that you have paid money for something that does not run on your device, has very poor resolution, has bugs (errors), or is an outdated version of the product.

Digital Plagiarism

Plagiarism is passing someone else's work off as your own. As long as there has been writing, people have been plagiarizing. But the Internet and downloadable devices have made it much easier to plagiarize written material. The Internet provides access to millions of documents, including a large number of research papers written by students and scholars. If you read

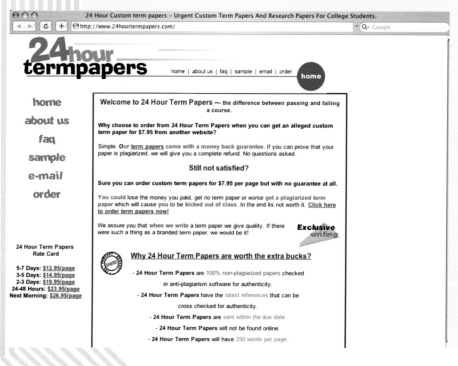

The Internet has many sites, such as 24 Hour Term Papers (www.24hourtermpapers.com), that sell prewritten papers.

a document and present the ideas in it as your own without crediting the original source, you are committing plagiarism. If you publish the material on your own Web site or as part of written work, the owner of the document can sue you for damages. The important thing to understand about plagiarism is that material does not have to be quoted exactly. If you pass off someone else's ideas as your own without crediting them, you are plagiarizing.

Downloading Papers

The Internet has made it much easier to purchase prewritten papers. In the past, some students cheated by paying other students to write papers for them. Digital technology has made it possible for students to buy papers more easily. Web sites for companies such as 24 Hour Term Papers and Research-Papers-On-Time sell their papers to anyone with a credit card. It is unethical (wrong) to download papers and attempt to pass them off as your own. It's also dumb. First, your teachers have a good idea of the type of work you've been doing. If you suddenly turn in something very different, they're likely to suspect that it's not your work. Moreover, both private and academic organizations provide tools that teachers can use to find out if a paper has been plagiarized or purchased. If you get caught turning in work that's not your own, you could face serious punishment such as failing a course, suspension from school, or getting expelled. There is no good reason to use the Internet services that provide prewritten papers.

Chapter 4

Protecting Intellectual Property

Make no mistake, companies work very hard to protect their intellectual property. This chapter looks at some of the steps that the U.S. government and industry organizations are taking to fight copyright infringement.

Types of Copyright Infringement

There are two categories of copyright infringement: direct and indirect. Direct copyright infringement occurs when a person uses copyrighted material in a way that is not allowed.

Indirect infringement occurs when you help others copy material that is copyrighted. One common example of indirect infringement is posting serial numbers or "unlock codes" on a Web site so that others can use software that has been copied illegally. Another example is providing software programs that break the copy protection on computer games or movie DVDs. It's illegal and unethical to pass along unlock codes, so don't do it. And don't think it's clever to come up with ways to get around copy protection on computer games—it could get you into a lot of trouble.

Digital Millennium Copyright Act

The Digital Millennium Copyright Act was passed in 1998. It addresses some of the new copyright infringement issues resulting from the Internet, wireless technology, and recording devices such as CD and DVD writers. Among other things, the law makes it a crime to provide tools to other people that allow them to illegally make copies of copyrighted material. It also provides guidelines and protections for those who have sites on which others post material. The act protects the person or company that owns the Web site from being held responsible if other people illegally post copyrighted material on the site, as long as the Web site owner follows guidelines outlined in the act.

Penalties for Copyright Infringement

Copyright infringers can be arrested and prosecuted. Criminal penalties for willful commercial infringement include imprisonment for up to five years and fines up to $250,000.

Millions of teens download songs over the Internet. However, making copyrighted songs available for downloading can result in serious penalties.

Copyright holders can also sue infringers in court to recover an amount equal to their losses, plus any profits made through the infringement (if bootleg copies are sold, for instance). In some cases, companies will also be awarded punitive damages by the court. "Punitive" means "punishing"; punitive damages are designed to punish a person for deliberately doing something wrong.

Recording Industry Crackdowns

Do you think that just because you're only a student, the big companies won't come after you for copyright infringement? Think again. Young people have not responded well to warnings and advertised messages intended to convince them that downloading copyrighted material is wrong. So now, the industry is taking a stronger stance and attempting to make students

A battle over fair use is being fought between users who want to download songs for their personal use and recording companies that want to protect their income from music sales.

realize that there are serious penalties for their misbehavior.

The Recording Industry Association of America (RIAA) represents major record companies in copyright cases. As early as 2002, the RIAA began bringing lawsuits against online consumers, including students. More recently, the RIAA began targeting students specifically. In February 2007, RIAA lawyers sent more than 400 letters to college students and staff members who they claim used campus computer systems

The Viacom vs. Google YouTube Lawsuit

The media company Viacom owns Paramount Pictures, the DreamWorks film animation studio, and several influential cable TV stations. Google is an Internet company that provides search engine services, allowing users to find information on the Internet. It also provides other services, including YouTube, which allows users to upload and download videos. In March 2007, Viacom filed a $1 billion lawsuit against Google. Viacom claims that close to 160,000 excerpts from films and videos owned by Viacom have been downloaded and viewed. It claims that YouTube allows the use of copyrighted properties without permission or payment to the copyright holder. Google claims that YouTube has respected the legal rights of copyright holders and that it provides a valuable service to media companies by providing them with the opportunity to promote their products to a large audience. One question is whether the use of the clips falls under "fair use" as defined by copyright laws. Fair use allows the copying of excerpts for criticism, comment, research, and reporting, as long as the excerpts are not sold. Google also claims that, according to the Digital Millennium Copyright Act, it is not guilty of copyright infringement as long as it removes copyrighted material from its Web site when it is informed of the problem. How this lawsuit is resolved will no doubt affect how other file-sharing sites behave in the future.

> This video is no longer available due to a copyright claim by Viacom International Inc.

Google displays this warning when it removes copyrighted material from its YouTube Web site. The company claims the warning protects it from being sued over material posted on its site.

to illegally share copyrighted songs. The letters offered the students the chance to settle the dispute, to avoid being sued. The purpose of suing individual students is to impress on students that downloading copyrighted music and movies without payment is theft, and they will be punished for it.

Software & Information Industry Association Crackdowns

The Software & Information Industry Association (SIIA) has also been working with computer services at colleges to combat the illegal copying and selling of software. The association has started a major effort to educate administrators about the need to combat this problem, and they are responding. For example, in 2006, computer services staff at one college noticed that usage on the computer network had more than tripled. They alerted the SIIA, which started an investigation that revealed that two students had set up Web pages on the system to illegally transfer software programs. The students were caught. The SIIA settled with the students on the condition that they provide the organization with information on where they obtained the illegal software. They also made the students perform community service—but the results could have been far worse for the students. Be aware that schools are more closely monitoring the usage of their computer systems and working actively to cut down on illegal usage.

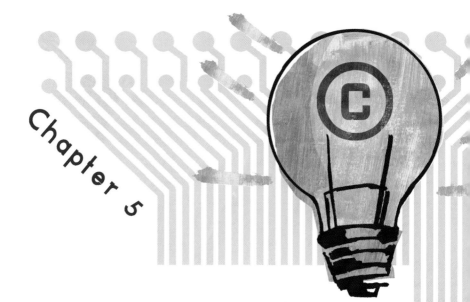

The Future of Intellectual Property Protection

The law is always changing to meet new challenges. This chapter looks at some new laws that have been proposed and new technologies designed to protect intellectual property.

The Intellectual Property Protection Act

As mentioned earlier, the distributing of unauthorized copies of copyrighted material costs major media companies billions of dollars each year. The scope of the problem has led to a demand for stronger laws to combat it. One such piece of legislation is the Intellectual Property Protection Act. This act is currently being considered by the U.S. Congress. It incorporates stronger penalties for copyright infringement and grants government investigators broader powers. Aspects of the act include the following:

This FBI anti-piracy seal is displayed on CDs and DVDs. The seal was released in 2004 as part of an FBI effort to crack down on piracy.

- It would increase the penalties for copyright infringement from five years to ten for the first offense and from ten years to twenty for additional offenses.
- It would let copyright holders seize documentation related to copyright infringement and would allow the government to take any property used by offenders in committing copyright infringement.
- It would create a special unit in the Federal Bureau of Investigation (FBI) devoted to dealing with copyright infringement. It would also permit the use of wiretaps (electronic listening devices attached to phones) in copyright infringement investigations.
- It would allow criminal penalties for copyright infringement to be applied even for work not registered in the U.S. Copyright Office.

- It would strengthen the law against distributing software or devices that enable people to copy and distribute unauthorized copies.

The Fair Use Act of 2007

Protecting intellectual property is clearly important. However, many feel that making stronger laws against copying interferes with the use of copyrighted material for reasonable purposes, such as research. To protect the "fair use" of copyrighted material, in 2007, Representatives Rick Boucher (D-VA) and John Doolittle (R-CA) submitted a bill to Congress called the Freedom and Innovation Revitalizing U.S. Entrepreneurship (FAIR USE) Act. They feel that the type of regulations that the large media companies are trying to obtain will make it difficult for people to use music, TV, and movies in their own homes. They also believe that it would hurt the ability of libraries to preserve (save) and archive (store) copyrighted material. The act would protect the rights of:

- Teachers to make copies of copyrighted works to use in the classroom
- Individuals to record programs for the purpose of skipping parts of them (such as commercials)
- Libraries to make copies to preserve material in their collections

- Reviewers and scholars to quote material for the purpose of review, criticism, or analysis
- Individuals to transmit files among their own home network of devices (for example, transferring files between one's notebook and home computer or between a home computer and an iPod)

New Technologies to Protect Intellectual Property

Software, audio, and video manufacturers attempt to protect their products by various means. In the past, some required users to type in a password or a product key sold with the disc or tape. But this type of protection has not stopped the copying and sharing of copyrighted discs. Therefore, manufacturers are developing new technologies that are harder to get around, including encryption. "Encrypted" means "in code." Using this technology, the digital material is stored in a coded form. In order to play the material, you must use a key to decode it. The key is available either on the playback device (such as a video game console like the Microsoft Xbox or Nintendo Wii) or on the purchased disc. In the latter case, the disc is manufactured so that the key is not copied if a user copies the information on the disc to another CD or DVD. This type of copy protection is designed to stop users from

New Technologies to Detect Plagiarism

Plagiarized papers have become a big problem in schools and colleges. Educators are fighting back, however. New technologies are being developed to detect plagiarism in students' work. One approach is document archives. Web sites such as Plagiarism.org, iThenticate.com, and Turnitin.com compile archives of documents from across the Web. Turnitin.com has compiled more than 15 million papers written by students. Teachers can log on to these sites and check the content of student papers against the archive to identify cases of plagiarism.

This approach comes with its own problems, however. At one Virginia high school, students rose up in protest when a teacher required them to run their papers through the Turnitin.com database to check for plagiarism. The students objected because of the "presumption of guilt" and refused to turn in their papers. In such cases, the students generally triumph. In addition, these school paper databases are being sued, ironically, for violating intellectual property laws! How is this possible? In the past, Turnitin.com added each checked paper to its archives, thereby expanding its database. Student authors claimed that this meant Turnitin.com was using their intellectual property for commercial purposes without crediting them. As of June 2007, the case was still being decided in the courts.

The Turnitin.com Web site (www.turnitin.com) provides a variety of "assessment tools" that may help teachers instantly identify papers containing unoriginal material.

purchasing one copy of a disc and making copies for their friends. Manufacturers are developing more complicated coding processes that will make it even harder for professional pirates to copy discs.

Respect for Intellectual Property

It is important to respect intellectual property rights and properly use copyrighted material because this will help ensure that it remains possible to use such material at all. It is also smart. It is getting harder and harder to get away with violating copyright holders' rights, and detection technologies are improving rapidly. Illegally copying and sharing copyrighted material can result in criminal prosecution, and the chances of getting caught are increasing all the time.

Glossary

archive To store a collection of material; or, the location in which a collection is stored.

bootleg copy Illegal copy of a DVD or CD.

bugs Errors in a file that cause it to perform incorrectly.

downloadable Able to be transferred from one computer to another.

ethical Relating to right and wrong.

excerpt Part selected from an entire work.

heir A person who inherits property.

impede To interfere with or slow the progress of.

laser A device that uses light to read and write information.

network A group of connected computers.

patron One who supports an artist financially.

preserve To save.

prosecution Being taken to court on a criminal charge by a state or federal law enforcement agency.

punitive Designed to punish.

reproduction A copy of something.

search engine A Web site that allows you to enter a word or phrase and find items on the Internet that relate to it.

virus A destructive program that affects the performance of a computer.

wiretap An electronic device that allows authorities to listen in on a person's telephone conversations.

For More Information

Canadian Intellectual Property Office
Place du Portage I
50 Victoria Street, Room C-114
Gatineau, Quebec K1A 0C9
Canada
Web site: http://strategis.ic.gc.ca/sc_mrksv/cipo/
    welcome/welcom-e.html

Entertainment Software Association
575 7th Street NW, Suite 300
Washington, DC 20004
Web site: http://www.theesa.com

Entertainment Software Association of Canada
130 Spadina Avenue, Suite 408
Toronto, ON M5V 2L4
Canada
Web site: http://www.theesa.ca

Motion Picture Association of America Anti-Piracy Office
One Executive Boulevard, Suite 455
Yonkers, NY 10701
(914) 378-0800
Web site: http://www.mpaa.org

Software and Information Industry Association
1090 Vermont Avenue NW, Sixth Floor
Washington, DC 20005-4095
(202) 289-7442
Web site: http://www.siia.net

U.S. Copyright Office
101 Independence Avenue SE
Washington, DC 20559
(202) 707-5959
Web site: http://www.copyright.gov

U.S. Department of Justice
Criminal Division (Computer Crime & Intellectual
    Property Section)
10th & Constitution Avenue NW
John C. Keeney Building, Suite 600
Washington, DC 20530
(202) 514-1026
Web site: http://www.cybercrime.gov/ccips.html

Web Sites

Due to the changing nature of Internet links, Rosen Publishing
has developed an online list of Web sites related to the subject
of this book. This site is updated regularly. Please use this link
to access the list:

http://www.rosenlinks.com/cccs/inpr

For Further Reading

Charmasson, Henri. *Patents, Copyrights, and Trademarks for Dummies*. Indianapolis, IN: For Dummies, 2004.

Francis, Barbara. *Other People's Words: What Plagiarism Is and How to Avoid It*. Berkeley Heights, NJ: Enslow Publishers, 2005.

Gordon, Sherri Mabry. *Downloading Stuff from the Internet: Stealing or Fair Use?* Berkeley Heights, NJ: Enslow Publishers, 2005.

Hart-Davis, Guy. *Internet Piracy Exposed*. Indianapolis, IN: Sybex, 2001.

McJohn, Stephen M. *Copyright: Examples and Explanations*. New York, NY: Aspen Publishers, 2006.

McJohn, Stephen M. *Intellectual Property: Examples and Explanations*. New York, NY: Aspen Publishers, 2006.

Menhard, Francha Roffe. *Internet Issues: Pirates, Censors, and Cybersquatters*. Berkeley Heights, NJ: Enslow Publishers, 2002.

Schwartau, Winn. *Computer and Internet Ethics for Kids*. Seminole, FL: Impact Press, 2001.

Torr, James D. *Internet Piracy*. Chicago, IL: Greenhaven Press, 2004.

Bibliography

Abdalla, Abdalla Ahmed. *International Protection of Intellectual Property Rights: In Light of the Expansion of Electronic Commerce*. Ph.D. thesis, self-published, 2005.

Boucher, Rick. "Reps. Boucher and Doolittle Introduce the FAIR USE Act." Press release. April 22, 2007. Retrieved May 1, 2007 (http://www.boucher.house.gov/index.php?option=com_content&task=view&id=1011&Itemid=75).

Bushweller, Kevin. "Generation of Cheaters." *American School Board Journal*, April 1999. Retrieved April 22, 2007 (http://www.asbj.com/199904/0499coverstory.html).

Fisher, William W., III. "The Growth of Intellectual Property: A History of the Ownership of Ideas in the United States." Harvard University. Retrieved April 22, 2007 (http://cyber.law.harvard.edu/property99/history.html).

"Music Piracy and the Audio Home Recording Act." *Duke Law & Technology Review*, January 20, 2002. Retrieved May 1, 2007 (http://www.law.duke.edu/journals/dltr/articles/2002dltr0023.html).

Pilon, Mary. "Anti-Plagiarism Programs Look Over Students' Work." *USA Today*, May 22, 2006. Retrieved May 29, 2007 (http://www.usatoday.com/tech/news/2006-05-22-plagiarism-digital_x.htm).

Recording Industry Association of America. "RIAA Pre-Lawsuit Letters Go to 22 Campuses in New Wave of Deterrence Program." Retrieved May 1, 2007 (http://www.riaa.com/news/newsletter/041107.asp).

Software and Information Industry Association. "Anti-Piracy."
    Retrieved May 1, 2007 (http://www.siia.net/piracy).

University of North Carolina at Chapel Hill. "Copyright
    Corner: Criminal Copyright Infringement." Retrieved
    May 20, 2007 (http://www.unc.edu/~unclng/copy-
    corner66.htm).

U.S. Congress. "H.R. 11." Retrieved May 28, 2007 (http://
    209.85.165.104/search?q=cache:F3SNMXGU1SwJ:action.
    eff.org/site/DocServer/boucher_hr_1201.pdf%3Fdocid%3
    D461+fair+use+act+2007&hl=en&ct=clnk&cd=1&gl=us).

U.S. Copyright Office. "Copyright: Fair Use." Retrieved
    May 15, 2007 (http://www.copyright.gov/fls/fl102.html).

U.S. Department of State. "Focus on Intellectual Property
    Rights." Retrieved April 22, 2007 (http://usinfo.state.gov/
    products/pubs/intelprp).

ZDNet. "Viacom Sues Google over YouTube Clips." Retrieved
    May 1, 2007 (http://news.zdnet.com/2100-9588_22-
    6166668.html).

Index

About the Author

Jeri Freedman has a B.A. from Harvard University. She is the author of eighteen young adult nonfiction books, many published by Rosen Publishing. Under the name Ellen Foxxe, she is the coauthor of two alternate history science fiction novels. She lives in Boston.

Photo Credits

Cover Les Kanturek; p. 6 © Oliver Stratmann/AFP/Getty Images; p. 9 www.earlyamerica.com/earlyamerica/firsts/copyright; p. 10 © Hulton Archive/Getty Images; p. 12 © www.istockphoto.com/Dragan Trifunovic; p. 14 © Timothy A. Clark/AFP/Getty Images; p. 19 © Peter Cade/Iconica/Getty Images; p. 20 © Jim Sugar/Corbis; pp. 23, 30 © AP Image; p. 31 © Nicholas Kamm/AFP/Getty Images; p. 35 © David McNew/Getty Images.

Editor: Christopher Roberts; **Photo Researcher:** Amy Feinberg